DIRTY LAUNDRY

DIRTY LAUNDRY

How Women Can Wash Away Destructive
Behaviors and Live Their Best Lives

HEATHER BIBLOW

Copyright © 2021 by Heather Biblow

All rights reserved.

No part of this book may be reproduced, or stored in a retrieval system, or transmitted in any form or by any means, electronic, mechanical, photocopying, recording, or otherwise, without express written permission of the Publisher or Author, with the exception of reviewers who may quote brief passages.

Limit of Liability: Neither the Publisher nor the Author make any representations, warranties, or guarantees, and stipulate that the advice, suggestions, opinions, and strategies contained in the book may not be suitable for every situation. The work is provided with the understanding that neither the Publisher nor the Author is rendering professional advice or services. Under no circumstances will any blame or legal responsibility be held against the Publisher or Author for any damages and/or monetary loss due to the information contained within this book, either directly or indirectly.

References are provided for informational purposes only and do not constitute endorsement of any websites or other sources. Websites listed in this book were live at the time of writing and may change.

ISBN: 978-1-7371923-1-2

Cover design by pro_ebookcovers

DEDICATION

This is dedicated to my Mother, Ann Biblow, who was and will always be the strongest, most intelligent, delightfully humorous, and independent woman ever. Her sheer determination to live life on her own terms inspired all who met her to want to be better versions of themselves.

CONTENTS

CHAPTER 1	Introduction	Page 1
CHAPTER 2	The Forces of Nurture	Page 10
CHAPTER 3	Step 1 – Mirrors Up!	Page 21
CHAPTER 4	Step 2 – Behavioral Assessment	Page 33
CHAPTER 5	Step 3 – Action Plan	Page 36
CHAPTER 6	Tawk To Me – Public Speaking	Page 45
CHAPTER 7	Additional Points	Page 57

CHAPTER 1: INTRODUCTION

FIRST, AN INTRODUCTION BECAUSE YOU DON'T KNOW ME

I am just like you – I am a work in progress. And even though I'm ~~old~~, ummm, seasoned, I make mistakes every day...EVERY DAY! But the wonderful truth about being a work in progress is that anyone can improve at any age, at any point in their careers or in their personal lives, and make a profound and positive impact on themselves, and of course, on others. And that's what happened to me.

After working for years in Air Traffic Control, I discovered I was becoming insignificant. I went from being an outgoing, gregarious, fearless, intelligent, successful, and occasionally bitchy person, to a Doormat! I was shying away from making scenes, allowing people to walk all over me, not speaking up and addressing abuses, and these behaviors were affecting both my professional and personal lives. I was a mess.

So, I went on a self-assessment journey to fix ME, and more importantly, to modify my responses to the behaviors of others that were negatively impacting me. I wrote this book to capture the methods I used for this self-improvement, in hopes that other women can benefit from my awakening. I hope my experience makes a positive impact for you.

◆◆◆

DIRTY LAUNDRY?

The term "Dirty Laundry" stems from the old adage "Don't air your dirty laundry," which means that a family never discusses its problems in public. And in many families, they didn't discuss it within the family either.

I'll put it into the context of my own situation: I purposely did not want to acknowledge the Dirty Laundry that controlled me and that was within me for fear that I would be upsetting the role and the boundaries that I, and mostly society, created for my life.

MY DEFINITION OF DIRTY LAUNDRY

Because of many factors, most being society-created norms for control, women are programmed to believe we are less valuable people, so we allow others to treat us in kind. We subconsciously put ourselves into subservient roles in our professional and private lives, and willingly accept second-class treatment. We are conditioned to accept this status, and therefore, we send out confirming signals that we are inferior, are worth less than others, and allow people, mostly men, to dictate our self-worth. When others use and abuse us, we internalize the situation and do nothing or worse yet, think we caused, invited, or deserved that abuse. We are programmed to think that our potential contributions, whatever they are, are less respected and of lesser importance.

MY AHA MOMENT

I initially recognized my own self-destructive behaviors when I purchased a single-family house. As a single woman buyer, the builder's representative treated me with a condescending attitude. I believe I received this less than acceptable treatment because of three reasons:

- This male-centric environment was created in order to control women,

- The builder's representative was banking on me not making a scene and not insisting that his company correct its errors, and

- We accept these roles because we think it's our lot in life.

I refer to this as my AHA Moment as it is the exact moment that I identified my own self-destructive tendencies that were permitting people to treat me like this and were so engrained in society that I bought into this.

◆◆◆

STARTING MY CAREER

Growing up, I neither thought, nor behaved, as if I had any limitations on my potential. I was born and raised in New Yawk City and assumed I could do anything. In fact, my chosen career field, Air Traffic Control, was an overwhelmingly male dominated profession but I never thought about it in those terms until my AHA moment.

I approached work believing that I belonged there from the first day, thanks to my Parents, whose support, encouragement, and in-your-face attitudes, set us up for success. Thanks also goes to my Sister whose continuous inspiration and mentoring made me want to do great things. And my attitude and sheer excitement at beginning my career probably helped to overcome any resistance I may have been subjected to, had my approach at work not been so positive from the start.

That was not the case with many of the other females at work. They faced very negative, overtly hostile reactions from their co-workers, much of it with sexual harassing undertones.

Most of my co-workers and team members were caring, supportive and inspiring, and treated me as an equal from the start. I was successful in certifying as an Air Traffic Controller because of their commitment to the job, their work ethic, their amazing personalities, and their generosity to all team members. My own hard work also was key to my success, something that women often forget to mention, acknowledge, or even realize.

After the interaction with the builder's representative, I began to question whether I had settled into a pacifist role both in my professional and personal lives. I had been in the workforce for almost 12 years by that point, but I must have been sending out an aura of insecurity, and people were starting to take advantage of it. I needed to figure out how to reverse this situation, fix ME, and make it clear to people that they do not have the right to treat me this way.

BUT WHERE TO START?

My experiences with that builder made me finally face a mirror and look at my own self-destructive behaviors, and the larger cultural environment that held women back. I did some soul searching, to try and figure out what I was doing, and what was causing me to exhibit these negative traits, but this was not an easy thing to do at first.

So, I concentrated on looking at and examining the actions of my friends, co-workers, noticing actions of strangers in stores, news reports, and paying attention to portrayals of women on TV. That helped me observe and identify, in greater detail, the behaviors of women in everyday situations, to see their attitudes as well as attitudes of other people towards women. And then it was easier to recognize behaviors that were adversely impacting me.

In thinking about these negative traits in more detail, I

realized these behaviors affect lots of women, as this accepted norm has been created and encouraged throughout the centuries. This pervasive attitude, however, can also affect those that are perceived to be 'different,' those who do not fit into the accepted mold.

IN THE PAST…

I frequently noticed what I thought were uncertain, insecure, apprehensive women prior to my AHA Moment. But this examination enabled me to see the underlying societal norms and condescending male behaviors that were, in large part, driving these traits. And I knew that it was more than just the difference between a New York vs. a non-New York upbringing.

YEESH!

Once I became more focused, I knew I couldn't change the world overnight, but I could start to make a difference in my own life. And perhaps in bringing it to the attention of others, I could make them see their role in this prejudiced environment.

Quite frankly, the behaviors I had bought into and exhibited were counter-productive to personal and professional success and were becoming a self-induced prison sentence. I was settling into a role designed by society, foregoing the potential within me. And when I started to examine what was holding me back, I realized that much of this impact was enforced by an environment that permeated everything I did, both at work, and in my personal life.

MY OWN METAMORPHOSIS

My builder event was my AHA Moment, and I realized I needed to change, but how? I had no clue as to how to take on this two-fold conundrum; the behaviors of others towards me and my own behaviors.

I initially started by conducting a self-assessment, as I needed to fully identify and understand what I was doing, and what other people were doing. After pinpointing these behaviors, I developed an action plan to start addressing my issues. I created a 3-step approach that turned into a metamorphosis that affects how I behave and how people interact with me.

I am amazed at how much more fulfilling my life is now that I don't settle for second-class status. I opened myself up to opportunities that I was shying away from and no longer believe that I am not worthy of success. As I continued to work on this, I realized...

I WAS NOT ALONE

My next AHA Moment came when a work colleague exhibited these same self-destructive traits. This colleague asked for my help in preparing her for a job interview. I had been in Air Traffic Control management for the 10+ years prior to that time and was delighted that she asked for my help. I then gathered my own thoughts on interview preparation techniques.

When we had our tutoring session, I posed some questions and explained the basic ones I always have answers at-the-ready for, should they come up in the interview. I suggested that she be prepared to respond to the "tell us about yourself" question that is inevitably asked.

SHE COULDN'T COME UP WITH A RESPONSE!

I was shocked. I reminded her that she has a lot to boast about, given her experience with air traffic operations, investigations, and evaluations (many times acting as the lead investigator) but she still could not come up with a response.

SHE WAS STUMPED, AND SO WAS I

Here was this very talented, very effective, outstanding managerial official, and she didn't think she had anything to offer. What made this situation worse was that at the time, she was temporarily employed as the acting manager in the actual position she was applying for and she was already receiving accolades for her performance in that role. Yet, she still doubted that she had an edge over her competition.

When I suggested that she look at the requirements of the job vacancy, and then include those required skills in the response to the resume question, she downplayed her contributions. I had to explain that she needed to look at her past jobs and suggested that she already possessed and demonstrated required skills for this position, many times over, and she needed to communicate that to the interview panel.

SHE DEGRADED HER OWN SUCCESSES

She told me she never thought about her experiences in that way before. She belittled her own self-worth and accomplishments as I believed she was preprogrammed to minimize her importance, capabilities, and skills. What was also remarkable was that I still had to specifically point out her skills before she started to see them herself.

From my vantage point, this colleague was far superior to most of her competition. She probably had the job locked-up because of her stellar performance during the temporary detail, and yet she still doubted that she had the GOODS.

After that encounter, I went home and thought about this type of predicament. Although I was only exploring and addressing what was causing me to exhibit these self-destructive behavior patterns, I realized that many women are severely impacted by this same conduct that sabotages their future potential.

Right then I decided to share my Dirty Laundry so that it

could help others. And if I could show how I modified my own behavior and how that resulted in significant changes to the behaviors of others towards me, many other women trapped in this negative merry-go-round could benefit from my experience.

I also include my primer on how to overcome public speaking fears (Chapter 6, "Tawk to Me"), as public speaking was the one overarching issue many women have told me stood in the way of their success. I created a quick and easy way to overcome those fears and taught this method to all types of audiences. I hope you find this primer helpful.

◆◆◆

WARNING BEFORE YOU PROCEED FURTHER

The reason I wrote this book is to help women. I hope this does that for you, but I must warn you in advance that you need to enter into this journey that this book will take you on with your eyes open. Because of what you will learn and how you will change and grow, and more importantly, demand change in other people's behaviors towards you, your world will be altered forever.

So before beginning the journey, have a serious discussion with yourself to make sure you are ready to air your own Dirty Laundry. And if the decision is YES...

CONGRATULATIONS!

I'm delighted that you are at that point in your life where you are ready to hold up that mirror. Here's hoping you can identify those self-destructive behaviors that work against you and do not allow you to experience ALL that life has to offer. And the best news is that these self-destructive and self-defeating behaviors are fully reversible. You're never too young, and never too seasoned, to change for the better.

DIRTY LAUNDRY

I hope you have a wonderful, cleansing trip to the Laundromat.

And by the way, my colleague got that job!

CHAPTER 2: THE FORCES OF NURTURE

SO HOW DID WE GET IN THIS SITUATION?

I struggled with this question. Here are some of my thoughts:

- Was it actually expected for women to assume these roles because it ensures we stay controllable?

- Do we present a threat to men or society if we go against the system they created where men are the domineering force?

- Is this expected behavior so engrained in society, or was it just something I was experiencing because I was refusing to be treated in such a fashion, or because I chose a career field that was historically a male dominated profession?

- Does a woman accept or even welcome this conditioning to limit her responsibilities on purpose?

HOW AND WHERE TO BEGIN

Before I could identify the destructive efforts in my world, I needed to fully understand the forces behind these behaviors and norms; what was the underlying foundation that encouraged me to exhibit these destructive behaviors, what created that accepted controlling environment? To that end, I developed a list of forces at play that seemed to have the greatest negative impact on me. I call these The Forces of Nurture!

And here's another warning – I wrote this book as a way to face some truths and make the lives of women better. When looking and analyzing those truths, the stark reality is that some of these forces aren't pretty. But I needed to include those ugly truths because education is required for self-realization. We need to understand these forces in order to start ensuring that they will not dominate our futures!

♦♦♦

THE FORCES OF NURTURE

1. Traditions:

I first looked at the family unit to see what role traditions play in setting women up for these behaviors. During my childhood, and in many families, women took on the role of nurturer. Even if they had careers outside the home, many were viewed as supportive roles in order to promote our children or men, rather than promote ourselves. Popular culture reinforced these stereotypical subservient roles for women.

The great news is that in today's world, families come in all shapes and sizes. Roles and family responsibilities are defined and redefined as dictated by family needs, or individual desires and goals, and this Force of Nurture may not be as limiting as it once was.

MY REALITY

What made this observation so confusing was that my actual family situation was very different. My Father was an amazing person, who believed that my Sister and I could do anything we wanted to. His encouragement and support enabled us to have careers that were both in primarily male dominated professions and were somewhat unusual, challenging career options.

My Mom was a pioneer for women, refusing to be controlled, defined, limited by men and society, and to this day her influence continues to foster a Women-Strong attitude in our family and friends. Because of this environment, I approached work believing that I belonged there from the first day.

Regardless of whether you grew up in a similar environment where family members were your personal champions, or in a polar opposite situation, you have to analyze, consider, and address this factor as it is still an underlying current in society. These centuries-old dictates have created a discriminating foundation that continues to impact women.

♦♦♦

2. Societal Norms:

I must start off this section by stating emphatically that the United States is the most wonderful country in the world, and I know how truly lucky and blessed we are to be living here. But several decisions made during the start of the United States were flawed and tainted by biases and prejudices. Gone unaddressed and condoned, these decisions materialized into discriminating norms. Prohibiting women from voting until 1920 is just one example of these discriminating decisions.

The mere existence of laws, regulations, policies and practices that treated and still treat certain people differently, solidifies the false belief that some people are inferior to others.

IMPLEMENTATION OF ADDITIONAL CONTROLS

Since the establishment of the U.S. government, additional restrictions continued to be established and re-defined, that at their essence, control women. These restrictions run counter to what we have been taught were the founding principles of this country – life, liberty, and the pursuit of happiness, as well as equal justice under the law.

Even when these restrictions have been somewhat lifted to be more inclusive, the environment is still filled with pitfalls that make sure women are not treated equal to men. Let me explain.

DECEPTIVE TECHNIQUES

The implementation of expanded inclusion for women actually exposes an underlying psychological game. The deception? A society, group, etc., initially excludes you, then 'allows' you to be promoted or become a member, or they provide you with rights you should have had all along, and what is your reaction? You are so grateful for the inclusion that you don't object to any still-present limitations, nor harbor ill will for the original exclusion.

Your status should NEVER have been an issue, yet that gets lost in your appreciation of their subsequent permission for you to join, or in the granting of equal rights, or to advance in your career. This reinforces the belief that you are inferior to others in the controlling group – you may eventually be included, but you're still seen as different, always. In addition, the members of the original group continue to use your initial exclusion as a subliminal edge over you.

Unfortunately, these inequity factors have determined how society as a whole, views the values of its people. Expected roles and responsibilities were pre-ordained and created barriers. A look at our history shows how engrained in our society our inferior status was, as women didn't possess rights even to vote, control our own lives, or receive equal pay.

PAY DISPARITIES

Pay inequity continues to negatively impact women. For example, the American Association of University Women's (AAUW) report on pay gaps[1] and the National Women's Law Center's Fact Sheet on wage gaps[2] noted that on average, women earn only 82% of what white, non-Hispanic men are paid for the same work. For women of color, the rates are worse.

They reported that Black women, and Native Hawaiian and Pacific Islander women are paid 63 cents on the dollar, Latinas earn 55 cents on the dollar, and Native American or Alaska Native women earn 60 cents on the dollar, when compared to every dollar made by white, non-Hispanic men. Asian women fare a little better at 87 cents, but it is still below what white, non-Hispanic men earn. AAUW added that these significant pay gaps also affect retirement incomes as the lower wages impact both pension and social security payouts.

Pay disparity not only impacts how a woman can financially support herself, her lifestyle, her family, her health, etc., it sends both a camouflaged and obvious message to everyone that a woman isn't worth as much as a man.

◆◆◆

---

[1] AAUW's The Simple Truth About the Gender Pay Gap, 2020 Update
[2] National Women's Law Center's The Wage Gap: The Who, How, Why, and What to Do, October 2020 Fact Sheet

3. Government And Management:

Until Affirmative Action laws were enacted to assist women and minorities to be competitive for employment, the labor workforce was not representative of the United States population. And despite those laws and associated requirements, high level management continued to resist selecting competent females for positions of power and authority. What I witnessed in the workplace during the initial push to hire women into managerial and executive levels gave the perception that these individuals failed when given the opportunities to advance.

SELF-FULFILLING PROPHECIES

From my perspective, many of the candidates selected for those early promotions lacked the necessary training, experience, or skills, and lacked the required mentoring and support. Was this by design? I wondered if the selecting officials promoted people destined for failure, on purpose, providing upper management with self-created evidence that women could not hold positions of power.

This concerted effort seemed to further erode confidence in promoting women. And although this occurred at the initial implementation of affirmative action initiatives, and there's been a few decades since that program attempted to help eliminate barriers for women to advance, gender discrimination exists today and still significantly limits a woman's ability to advance in the workforce.

❖❖❖

4. Sexual, Physical and Other Intimidating Behaviors:

These are serious issues that make women take a back seat to men. They include:

- Sexual Harassment

- Sexual/Physical Assault

- Other Intimidating Behaviors

SEXUAL HARASSMENT: This type of harassment is used for power and control, and still exists despite laws that prohibit it, and the implementation of training programs aimed at preventing sexual harassment. The underlying and most times not-so-subtle tolerance of women being sexually harassed or discussed as sexual objects demeans and degrades women and further creates untenable barriers, and uncomfortable, unsafe conditions for women.

Many abusers and predators have used their professional positions, power, and standing to harass women, but it occurs outside of the work environment as well. This pervasive, poisonous environment continues to attempt to control, mistreat and sabotage women.

SEXUAL/PHYSICAL ASSAULT: Rape and physical assault on females remain a real and present danger at the hands of acquaintances, co-workers, strangers, family.

When the assault occurs in the workplace, powerful men use their positions of authority to control, assault and attack women, and their influence fosters the underlying Dirty Laundry atmosphere. Many victims remain silent for years for a variety of reasons.

Recent events may provide women with a safer environment to speak out about these sexual assaults, such as the #MeToo movement[3] and other efforts. While the current state is promising, these dangers have had a profound impact on women for centuries.

---

[3] Metoomvmt.org

OTHER INTIMIDATING BEHAVIORS: The objectification of women by men also undermines our talents, effectiveness, equal standing, and minimizes our contributions to society. Examples of these include internet postings that rate women on superficial factors, using physical attributes to dismiss and deem women as insignificant and unimportant.

The outcome? A man's actions are viewed as effective, assertive, powerful; a woman's similar actions are viewed as pushy, aggressive, nasty. These types of condescending and chauvinistic comments are meant to bully and demean women. It is also done to send dog-whistle messages to other men that inappropriate behavior towards women is condoned, appropriate, and sanctioned.

◆◆◆

5. Personal Qualities:

This section focuses on how some women exhibit personalities that maintain a passive or docile posture. I believe that these qualities broadcast insecurity. They could also indicate a reluctance to challenge the status quo.

COMMUNICATION STYLES: I couldn't help but notice that many women have communication characteristics that undermine their effectiveness. For example, the mild-mannered way in which many women communicate – does it give the perception of weakness and insecurity? Do women communicate in a soft, billowy voice because society views that as being more feminine? Is this a natural tendency, or do women unconsciously adopt this mode of communication because we are programmed to think this is appropriate?

Some of these undermining communication characteristics I've observed include:

- Speaking in girlish, soft, wispy tones, and voice trails off toward the end of sentences

- When referring to things we do or have, women often use the descriptor "little"

- Ending sentences with raised inflection, rendering the gravity of statements inconsequential, or sounding like questions, instead of answers or statements

- Apologizing for things not our fault

- Hand over Mouth*

* I need to explain my last-mentioned point, Hand over Mouth, since this physical gesture seems so prevalent in many women's reactions to a majority of situations. I have noticed that many women (including me) react to events by covering up our mouths with our hands. It occurs when we are excited, horrified, shocked, laughing, happy, sad, embarrassed, outraged, pissed-off, angry, in disbelief, bored or even when we are disinterested.

I'm not convinced that I truly understand the 'why' of this gesture, but I think it could be for many reasons. Perhaps it is because we are afraid of showing emotions, are embarrassed, are behaving in a perceived lady-like manner, or, to state the obvious, hiding.

I have not seen similar actions from men for the most part, either in real life settings, or when portrayed by actors, so I do think this is primarily a female attribute. And when it occurs, I think it broadcasts a message of weakness or insecurity.

NON-ASSERTIVE STYLE: On a related note, I've noticed that some women have an unnatural impulse to show a gentle, non-aggressive, non-assertive demeanor, to their detriment. Are we programmed to believe that if we break out of that mold, and show an assertive side, we will not be seen as Ladies? I'm not sure why many women refuse to take on the alpha role, but I think this factor runs the risk of rendering them 'sheep' following the leader. It also sends a message of weakness or reluctance to assertively address issues.

◆◆◆

6. Lifestyles - Messages:

Over the last decade, a subtle message seems to have seeped into the mainstream of American life. This mantra is now so engrained it has permeated everything we do. The message: Children First!

Yes, adults are 100% responsible for the safety, welfare and healthy growth and development of their children, but somehow that changed into something else. The shift to children over all else sends the underlying message that adults are dispensable and are there only to serve and support children. Women take the brunt of that message, and when the mantra became "Children First," unfortunately I believe the silent but real message became "Women Last."

◆◆◆

FINAL THOUGHTS ON THE FORCES OF NURTURE:

These six categories are what I came up with. Use them as a foundation to start thinking about your world – are there other forces at work that you see affecting you and your ability to succeed? You may not agree with my categories, but to me, these define the environment that impacts my behavior. You need to identify the forces that negatively impact you.

CHAPTER 3: STEP 1 MIRRORS UP!

(I'M DOING WHAT?)

CAN I POSSIBLY CHANGE THE WORLD?

After considering my Forces of Nurture categories, I initially thought that there was no way one person could change the societal shackles that were holding women back. In rethinking this situation, I knew I could make a difference in several ways:

1. Advocate

2. Regulate

3. Change my Individual World

Women can advocate and enact laws and regulations that create a more supportive and fairer environment. And women can also become advocates for themselves and be the conduit for others to act. Here's what I did to change my world: I created a 3-step plan to start correcting behaviors.

THE PLAN

Step 1 – Mirrors Up, or I'm Doing WHAT?

Step 2 – Behavioral Assessment; Identifying your most prolific negative behaviors or your conditioned responses to external behaviors

Step 3 – Action Plan; Simple Steps approach to correct and eliminate destructive behaviors

◆◆◆

CONFESSION TIME:

Here's the truth about the 3-step plan

Most of your learning will come as a result of you consciously thinking about the Forces of Nurture to identify the societal barriers facing you, as well as the results of the exercise in Step 1, to identify your actions and the actions of others that hold you back. That's what happened to me – once I became aware of what I was doing to sabotage myself, or allowing, even welcoming the actions of others to dictate my behaviors, life became easier and less stressful. My dreams and visions of what I wanted to accomplish were clarified and sharpened and attainable.

However, I still recommend completing the other steps, especially for those struggling with how to correct these behaviors. But understand that half the learning is identifying and being aware of the problems and their root causes standing in the way of your potential.

GOOD NEWS: Contrary to popular belief, it does not take seven years to change a habit. But it can only happen once you consciously decide to make a change. When you know exactly the 'what' and the 'why' and the positive transformation it will make for you if you address it, it's so simple to make a profound change.

◆◆◆

STEP 1 ACTIVITY:
MIRRORS UP! (I'm Doing WHAT?)

You have to create a List of your behaviors and the behaviors of others that impact you negatively, and the only way to do this is to hold a mirror to your individual situations. Start to identify if you have problems getting noticed at school or work, or you do not get the recognition that you deserve, or you get inferior service or treatment.

As I started to build my List, it actually became an enjoyable activity because I was seeing myself differently, almost from a third-person's perspective. The pivotal key for me was to look at the individual situations I had during the day. I call this my 'Doormat List.'

LET'S GET STARTED...

Get out your laptop, your tablet, your planner, a cocktail napkin, or just a pad of paper, and create your own Doormat List. Write down any item that defines your behavior or your situation, and the actions of others toward you.

To assist you, I updated my personal Doormat List by adding lots of observed actions and supplemented it with nuances that didn't exist back when I went through this process. These include such things as the wide proliferation of social media.

This expanded List will help to open up your eyes to possible situations that impact you. This List is long and detailed, but it is still not all-encompassing. However, it should contain enough examples for you to begin creating your own personal List, which will be different from mine.

START by looking at your daily world for several weeks and write down the observed negative behaviors every day. Document how your interactions happened and the resulting outcomes of those events. And especially include the actions, reactions, non-verbal messaging of the people you interacted with, and what the associated impact was on you or others.

A word of caution: To create your own Doormat List, you can design oodles of spreadsheets, inter-connected forms, use apps, deploy macros, etc. But the reality is that this is not about the format you use – it is about consciously identifying and having an honest look at what others are doing to you, or what you are doing that is counter to realizing your greatest individual potential. Use or create whatever aids you want that make this effort easier and more effective for you, but don't let the format get in the way of the more important work, that being an objective observation of behaviors.

◆◆◆

THE DOORMAT LIST

A – Your Own Actions:

1. I never complain, and accept and expect secondary treatment

2. I cannot accept praise and responsibility for successes, and always belittle my accomplishments

3. I'm a martyr, always suffering and sacrificing for the good of others, whether a small, insignificant issue, or a larger, profound, self-impacting effort

4. I speak in a wispy, girlish voice, and do not finish sentences

5. My sentences or statements sound like they are questions since I raise my voice at the end

6. When talking on the phone, I'm almost apologetic when hiring service companies

7. When I refer to things I do or I have, I often use the descriptor "little"

8. I use Hand over Mouth reactions

9. I expend a great deal of energy trying to convince people that my accomplishments are meaningless, or substandard, or of lesser importance than the accomplishments of others

10. I don't correct someone who has misspoken, as I don't want to make anyone appear ignorant, even at the risk of making myself seem ignorant

11. I don't take an active role in retirement planning, or other financial matters, as I look to others and allow them to make the decisions for me, to my financial disadvantage

12. I sweep things under the rug rather than address the abuse

13. I constantly apologize, say I'm sorry, mostly for things that are not my fault

14. I do not speak up for myself

15. I abhor being the center of attention, will not make scenes and will do anything to keep the limelight away from me, to my detriment

16. I am introverted and shy, and use that as justification to not speak up, take actions or attain my goals

B – Actions Of Others:

1. Stereotypical lies have existed for centuries and cause men to see women as the weaker and dumber sex

2. Men assume that women do not know much, and assume any input I have is worthless

3. Men exclude and dismiss women because they think they have a license to do so

4. People try to take advantage of me because they assume I will not challenge them

5. They treat me as if I'm invisible, or insignificant

6. People abuse me because they think they can, and believe I won't fight back, won't complain, will not tell others

7. Their abusive behavior is both learned and condoned by their leaders, parents, management, news, social media, etc.

8. Men in high positions of power use personal attacks that undermine women (weight, looks, assumed low intelligence) and continue patterns of hurtful speech to mock, control and suppress women including use of crude and outrageous sexual references

C – At Restaurants:

1. I never get seated in the prime section, such as by windows with water views. I usually get a table in the worst section, closest to the kitchen, the restrooms, or the wait-staff's station

2. I do not get the same level of service that the table of men sitting across from me receives

3. I never complain if the food tastes bad, not what was ordered, or service is inferior

4. On the very rare occasion when I am asked if 'this' table is acceptable, even when it isn't, I never speak up and say it isn't

5. I do not order exactly what I want and settle for lower-priced items

6. I lie and tell the wait-staff that I haven't decided on my meal selection yet, so that I can order last after hearing what everyone else is ordering. I do this so that I don't order something that's too different or more expensive than what others order

D – At The Store:

1. Ignored by store service personnel

2. The clerk runs over to assist a male shopper even though I was there first, and I do not correct this

3. Merchants assume that I'm merely window-shopping, especially in high-ticket item shops

4. I will not ask for a refund on an item I bought that turned out to be damaged because the sign says 'no refunds' or because I do not want to create a scene

5. I stand and watch the cashier throw and crumble my purchases into a bag, without saying a word about this mishandling of my merchandise

6. I let others bust in line in front of me without speaking up

7. At the Bank, I need a co-signer (this is changing)

8. At the Home Improvement store, I'm invisible

9. Even if there's no one else in line ahead of me, I will still walk through the maze to get to the front of the waiting area for the next teller/server/cashier, in lieu of walking around to the front of the line directly

10. I observe locally-set rules without thinking 'why' or 'why not' – I never question these and sheepishly comply without thinking

E– At The Office:

1. People at work meetings treat me as if I'm invisible and steal my ideas by paraphrasing the suggestion I made earlier, without acknowledging me

2. I do not get to present my work to the bosses

3. I get paid less than my male counterpart although we are doing the same work

4. I was sexually harassed several times by a co-worker, and laughed it off because I felt embarrassed, rather than report it

5. My supervisor made a joke over something I did in front of my co-workers

6. My male co-worker makes derogatory comments about a female co-worker's looks, weight, and I and others do nothing

7. I think that my project and work product are inferior to what others accomplish

8. I do not have access to the informal communication flow and it negatively impacts my career progression by not being in-the-know

9. Even though I'm supposed to be an equal team member, I am consistently asked to take the notes/minutes

10. I agree to take notes at meetings even though no male co-worker is ever asked to do this task

11. I do not speak up at business meetings for fear of looking foolish or stupid

12. I have ideas for improvement, but am reluctant to bring them forward

13. I hit my glass ceiling

14. I do not have a mentor, and no one has asked me to mentor them

F – At Home:

1. As the Mother, my needs always come last

2. My career goals are usurped by my husband's job requirements

3. My brother is told he could be a corporate executive, I am told what a lovely assistant I will make

4. I take the blame for a problem in order to make peace in my marriage, relationship, family

5. I do not bring things to the attention of my relatives for fear that I'll upset the delicate balance

6. I clear up the table and do the dishes, while the males in my family retire to the family room and watch TV

G – At School:

1. My guidance counselor suggests I look towards historically women-oriented careers, even though I explain I want to go into aviation

2. I was assigned a Home Economics class as a required class, the boys were not

3. I am not called upon by the teacher to take a lead role

4. The plays we present have women in stereotypical, supportive roles

5. I would not raise my hand although I know the answer

6. Posts on social media make derogatory remarks about me or other girls

7. I was bullied

8. I saw other girls being bullied, and did nothing

H – Social Events:

1. I congregate only with people I know or people I sense are shy

2. I never actively engage in dialogue – rather, I engage via a listen-only mode

3. I shy away from being the center of attention

4. Rather miss out on opportunities than risk making a scene

5. I will never get up and dance in front of other people

6. I cannot approach powerful people

7. I never walk into a room with confidence; I usually trail behind someone

8. I stand with shoulders hunched inward, head down, and arms crossed in front of my body, not because it is a comfortable stance for me, but rather to feel more protected and hidden

I – Other Venues:

1. I will not challenge a doctor, dentist, or other professional, and never question treatment, procedures, or strategy although I have significant unanswered questions about what they are proposing, I am having horrible side effects, or I disagree with them

2. At the car dealership, I am given a significantly smaller trade-in allowance than the fair market value, and charged an inflated price for the new car

3. At the car service center, I'm talked down to and always charged hundreds of dollars for work that never seems logical to me, and I never question them

4. At the Hotel, I am assigned a small, noisy room, although my male traveling co-workers are given much better accommodations

5. At Church, the Elders, who set policies, are all men

6. There are substantial repairs in need of immediate addressing in my rental, and the owner, managing agent, keeps putting me off, and will not fix issues

7. At my new home, the builder keeps putting me off instead of just fixing my problems the right way the first time, or insisting there were no problems

CHAPTER 4: STEP 2 BEHAVIORAL ASSESSMENT

IDENTIFYING YOUR MOST PROLIFIC NEGATIVE BEHAVIORAL ATTRIBUTES

When I finished my Doormat List, the totality of harmful behaviors was overwhelming. I had absolutely no formal education in psychology or psychiatry, but I thought if I kept reviewing my List some generalities would start to emerge, and they did. I identified six behaviors I kept 'seeing.'

These six prominent traits or attributes described the majority of my actions and my conditioned responses to external behaviors. To further clarify them, I developed my own short definition of each.

The more I looked at those definitions, the more they started to get blurred, and I realized that several of them dealt with the same or very similar behavioral traits. However, looking at them in this fashion allowed me to break them down into truncated attributes that let me determine how to start correcting them.

When you review your Doormat List to come up with your individual attributes, do not get too worried if you have no formal psychological training either. If your Attribute list makes sense to you and allows you to start addressing your conduct and the behaviors of others in a way that is effective for you, that's all that matters. Then you can start to develop an action plan to address barriers to your success.

Lesson Learned: One thing I realized is that you are who you are perceived to be, and not necessarily who you think you are. These Behavioral Attributes were standing in the way of who I really wanted to be.

◆◆◆

STEP 2 ACTIVITY: BEHAVIORAL ASSESSMENT

This assessment will be the basis for developing a plan to address your issues and will make you aware of these situations in the future. Now that you have your individual Doormat List, you need to do that attribute assessment of your own List, so you can create your Action Plan.

I have provided my Attribute List below, as an example for you to consider. These represent the six different types of negative behaviors I was exhibiting, or I was subjected to.

◆◆◆

MY ATTRIBUTES

SUBSERVIENT – Here to serve others and not be the important person in the group.

SCENE – Shy away from creating scenes. Don't want the attention. Will suffer or sacrifice anything in order not to be the center of attention.

SELF-ESTEEM – Believe you're lower than dirt. Don't deserve anything good. Not worthy of being the first or the best. No confidence.

SETTLE – Not good enough for the best, so mediocre or less is okay for me.

SUPPORT – Are the proverbial "Sacrificial Lamb" and are the chosen martyr. Do things only for the good of others, and your role in life is to help raise that other person up to their potential.

ABUSE – Believe you deserve mistreatment.

It's your turn to review your Doormat List several times, and start thinking about any commonality of your behaviors, or the behaviors of others and develop your Attributes. Remember to include a definition of each.

OKAY, WE'RE ON A ROLL, WHAT'S NEXT?

You now need to go back through your Doormat List, and denote which Attribute aligns to each Doormat item. Once each Doormat item has an associated Attribute, add up how many items are related to that one, and then identify your top two behavioral characteristics (Attributes). You can go back at a later date to address the others but starting with the two Attributes that occur the most makes sense, and it creates a manageable plan.

This is not scientific - the ranking of these Attributes created a practical way for me to initiate an action plan, and to be aware of common, related behaviors, and allowed me a way to initiate changes in my environment. If you want to start with only one, that's fine, too, but start with your most prolific negative behavior.

CHAPTER 5: STEP 3 ACTION PLAN

SIMPLE STEPS APPROACH

FEAR FACTOR: My approach was to use Simple Steps to address two significant fear factors when dealing with change:

1. Make changes to my own behaviors by making small, daily, incremental behavioral changes, and

2. Use positive approaches to make it palatable for others to modify their behaviors towards me and others, and to treat me appropriately.

When I started to look at how I needed to alter my own behaviors, I initially got confused because I wanted to fix things immediately and completely, and that kind of instantaneous transformation never happens. Well, it can happen, but the change probably won't be lasting.

I realized that in order for the changes to be effective, they needed to be small, incremental modifications so I could adopt them easier. Then I could build upon them with additional changes until the new effective behaviors became my normal conduct. With that acknowledgment, it became uncomplicated and much more straightforward to create fixes that would be effective in bringing about a lasting change in my own behaviors.

The second point in my Fear Factor approach, making others change their inappropriate behaviors towards me, may be fraught with difficulty in today's adversarial environment. Violence in the workplace, restaurants, public areas, and unfortunately, the home, are everyday occurrences in our world today. So, to enact these changes, I had to make it palatable for the receiver to actually 'hear' my statements.

THE HARSH REALITY

In my personal life, and in business, I observed that when people are faced with controversy, they often respond by becoming aggressive. Further, that aggressiveness can quickly change to anger. When that happens, they are no longer hearing what is being said, and it is usually met with total resistance or worse. Therefore, I knew I had to address the behaviors of others in a positive, honest, assertive, and effective manner.

Don't get me wrong. There were many situations where the necessary reaction to someone being rude or condescending was to aggressively call them out on it and embarrass them...the good old days. As a general rule, this was not and is still not the most advantageous and effective way to approach these issues, however, there is much to be said for stopping a Bully in their tracks!

You will have to assess your own situations to figure out how best to start correcting them, and if you need help, get it immediately.

Here are some considerations I used when determining how best to address others:

- Directly confront the person without piling on emotion, history, baggage

- Put that person on notice that their behavior is inappropriate

- Allow the person to correct their behavior without embarrassing them

- Explain the impact their actions have on you (and others)

- State that their behavior is eating away at their own effectiveness and reputation

- Request (demand) what you want them to do to correct their behaviors

- Raise the issue with others, when/if appropriate

- If the situation is unsafe, scary, harassing, etc., seek help from others immediately

- File a complaint, take legal action, document the abuse, as you deem appropriate

❖❖❖

STEP 3 ACTIVITY: ACTION PLAN

Beginning with the first Attribute you want to work on, think about what the continuation of this negative behavior does to you, so you can understand the impact it is having over you.

Next, look over your associated Doormat List items for that Attribute. Pick two that 'speak to you' – choose one that involves your behavior, and one that is caused by someone else's. Think about the simplest thing you can do to correct this behavior, or rather to start to correct it.

My Process: To develop an effective plan, I first needed to analyze and dissect the problem to ensure the root causes were identified. Then I concentrated on generating measures to address the problem, which included brainstorming lots of possible ideas. As an example, below is a detailed outline addressing one of my Attributes, Self-Esteem.

Specifically, this Doormat item under Self-Esteem is:

When talking on the phone, I'm almost apologetic when hiring service companies.

To address this issue, I would consider the following steps to figure out how I will correct this issue:

1. Strategy for this Doormat item: I would select a non-complex, uncomplicated issue to address first, such as a call to initiate a temporary newspaper hold. My second event would be a bit more challenging, perhaps a call to ask for a refund for a purchase that arrived broken. My third event would be to hire service people for a home repair.

2. Before calling, I'd write down talking points, verbatim, to include what the problem or issue is, what I want fixed, accommodated, and questions on when, how, and how much it will cost. (Action Plan should contain the actual talking points, etc.)

3. Practice the script in the mirror prior to calling, making sure to concentrate on maintaining a level-toned voice without a raised inflection, and staying true to the script. This practice can stop someone from projecting insecurity and uncertainness to the person being called, and will present someone who is confident, smart and a force to be reckoned

with. (Action Plan should include processes to prepare for the actual call.)

4. During the call, use a physical trick as a constant reminder to concentrate on voice quality and adherence to talking points. Loosely tying a string on your finger or applying a band-aid on your hand does work.

SUGGESTION: As you begin to work on your Action Plan, use the above process as a guide to help you navigate through it. When I am working to solve Dirty Laundry issues that still present themselves, I continue to use this detailed process to start the juices flowing to come up with possible ways to address issues.

To provide you with more examples, below is a sample Action Plan that takes on six different challenges, half concern other people's behaviors and half concentrate on mine.

◆◆◆

ACTION PLANS TO ADDRESS BEHAVIORS

(SAMPLES, SUGGESTIONS)

1. <u>ATTRIBUTE: SELF-ESTEEM</u> (My Actions):

BEHAVIOR: I cannot accept praise and responsibility for successes, and always belittle my accomplishments.

ACTION PLAN: Just say "Thank You" and then STOP TALKING!! Do not say anything else because that will downplay successes. Resist the urge to say anything else.

2. <u>ATTRIBUTE: SELF-ESTEEM</u> (Their Actions)

BEHAVIOR: At the Hotel, I am assigned a small, noisy room, although my male traveling co-workers are given much better accommodations.

ACTION PLAN: Upon arrival at the Registration desk, affirmatively state you want a room overlooking xxx and for safety reasons, not on a low floor, or whatever types of accommodations you prefer.

STRATEGY: Assertively ask for what you want upfront. That puts people on notice that you deserve and expect appropriate and good service from them. It is establishing how they approach you from the start, and how you proactively communicate with people.

3. **ATTRIBUTE: SETTLE** (My Actions)

BEHAVIOR: I agree to take notes at meetings even though no male co-worker is ever asked to do this task.

ACTION PLAN: If asked while at the meeting, calmly state that for fairness, someone else needs to perform this task.

STRATEGY: If/When you are more comfortable to address this situation, approach this in a meeting with your manager. You can raise these issues, as you deem appropriate:

* The fairness question
* Impacts your ability to fully engage in the meeting
* Adversely affects your work performance
* Undermines your level-playing field with your contemporaries
* Sexist

4. **ATTRIBUTE: SETTLE** (Their Actions)

BEHAVIOR: At the restaurant, I never get seated in the prime sections, such as by the windows with water views.

ACTION PLAN: Tell the Host, Hostess, Maître d' that you

prefer a water view, or xxx, and do this when they greet you at the door or at the front Host/Hostess station.

STRATEGY: Be up front about your desired location, and not after being seated at a less than acceptable table location. Don't add emotion, and just state calmly and directly what you want.

5. **ATTRIBUTE: SCENE** (My Actions)

   BEHAVIOR: Ignored by store service personnel.

   ACTION PLAN: Bring the slight or oversight to their attention. Start by addressing simple things at first, in a venue that is small.

   STRATEGY: If it's the case of being ignored as they assist the male patron, bring it to their attention that you were here first, once they do approach you.

   LESSON LEARNED: Next time you should be confident enough to bring this to their attention at the start of the oversight so you will be served first. **OOPS – here's the lesson:** Once I started to do this exercise, I did it by rote so quickly and wasn't fully observing the actual situation. I failed to realize that the person they 'appeared' to be giving preferential treatment to was, in fact, someone that was waiting in the wings for additional information in order for the salesperson to finalize their transaction. NEVER ASSUME you know the true/whole situation, so that is another lesson as to why and when and how you address behaviors of others. You must always keep it assertive and positive, and don't assume intent until the other person shows you their actual discriminating intent.

6. ATTRIBUTE: SCENE (Their Actions)

BEHAVIOR: People at work meetings treat me as if I'm invisible and steal my ideas by paraphrasing the suggestion I made earlier, without acknowledging me.

ACTION PLAN: Speak up as soon as the Idea-Stealer talks and call him/her on it by stating, without emotion, "this is a restatement of my earlier suggestion, that shows we are in agreement, which is great and now I'd like to hear if others support this idea too."

STRATEGY: It will embarrass the Idea-Stealer but will be done without hostility on your part and put the others on notice. A positive way to change behaviors and still continue to push the work forward collaboratively.

◆◆◆

FOLLOW-UP ACTIVITY:

As I mentioned, I started off this whole process of self-improvement in the Simple Steps manner to make it easier to incorporate slightly modified behavioral changes progressively. To do that, I prepared for the next day's events, by prepping myself the night before. Only then was I able to start to feel a comfort level because of my 'homework.' I also believe that unless you implement continuous improvement processes, you are doomed to slide back into your old, ineffective ways.

YOUR PLAN: You need to adopt review-and-preview time every day to ensure progression and to modify your plans, when and if required. This should also include a quick review of events, right after they occur, to assess your actions and the actions of others, and if you were able to modify behaviors to align with your action plan. If not, you need to figure out what you could have done to have made it more effective, and then alter your action plan to incorporate these changes.

If you are finding it hard to speak up even when you have created and memorized key talking points for the event, then your action plan should be changed to make your proposed talking points smaller, simpler and less scary for you. It's more effective to go slower if that's what you need to do. I also recommend you read Chapter 6 which will help you to overcome public speaking fears with a very easy-to-implement approach that will help you to find your voice.

This part of the Follow-Up Activity is CRITICAL! You are using every day to improve, as you're turning missed opportunities into learning sessions. Do not beat yourself up because you missed an opportunity to address someone's behavior or your own, and realize that this review process will help you to get it right the next time and be even more confident in your approach.

Once you start to modify behaviors, you also need to continue to address your other Doormat List items, until you are comfortable that you are policing yourself constantly. Until you have reached that point, you need to reassess your progress, at least daily at first and then periodically, to ensure you are getting better. Whatever your timeframe, you must commit to doing this.

CHAPTER 6: TAWK TO ME PUBLIC SPEAKING

HOW TO OVERCOME PUBLIC SPEAKING FEARS QUICKLY AND EASILY

EVERYONE hates to speak in public. Many people admit that they fear death less than they fear giving a speech, which seems somewhat extreme. But with some preparation and practice, you can become an effective raconteur.

What's your story – does the thought of getting up in front of an audience, and giving a speech, send chills throughout your body? Do you come up with outrageous excuses, such as considering elective surgery, to get out of a work presentation?

Well, according to Roscoe Drummond, and others that have been credited with versions of this quote, "The mind is a wonderful thing. It starts working the minute you are born, and never stops until you get up to speak in public."[4]

OH, PERFECT!

The stark reality is that everyone has to be at least comfortable with conversations, regardless of the size of the audience, in order to function and communicate effectively, whether for your professional or your private life. But most people believe that learning how to improve public speaking prowess is a

---
[4]toastmasters.org, Toastmaster magazine, February 2016

complicated, lengthy, sometimes expensive and always an uncomfortable process…but it's NOT!

I didn't start out with public speaking fears. I was extremely extroverted growing up, and actually looked for ways to be noticed, but somewhere along the way, I lost that nerve, that showmanship, and the fear of public speaking set in. I needed to figure out a way to overcome the panic that started building inside me because it was negatively affecting me at work. I was missing out on advancing because of this fear.

I noticed that this was affecting me personally as I was also shying away from everyday conversations. I wouldn't speak up in crowds or in one-on-one chats. I was becoming a piece of wallpaper.

To eliminate my fear of speaking in public, I designed a method to address this in a realistic way. I created a process that is uncomplicated and based on implementing progressive changes, that over time, would help me regain and improve upon my public speaking skills.

I wrote this primer as a result of holding lots of training sessions, instructing others on my solution. Many of the participants commented that my method was straightforward and ingenious, and they couldn't wait to start putting these measures in place for themselves.

I have included it in Dirty Laundry, as I believe that the fear of public speaking is one of the major causes that stop women from advancing, standing up for themselves, demanding equal treatment. In this chapter, I include much of the syllabus that I created for my class on how to overcome public speaking fears. Once you are more comfortable with this, everything else will be easier.

THE ESSENCE OF THE PROBLEM

Why is public speaking an issue? Is it because you:

- Do not want to make a scene
- Do not want to be the center of attention
- Do not want to be judged
- Have little faith in your own abilities
- Are afraid of failure
- Are afraid of success

WHAT IS THE ISSUE?

Regardless of what demotivates you, at the core of the problem is one thing that you need to work on, in small, incremental steps. That 'thing'?

You have to become comfortable hearing the sound of your voice in public.

HUH? THAT'S IT? Yes, that is it! And the way to address it is just as clear:

You need to use every opportunity to hone your speaking skills, by using any interaction, chat, chance meeting, to practice and improve those skills.

GENERAL PRINCIPLE: This method is designed around making you progressively more comfortable hearing the sound of your voice in public. The basic principle is to take advantage of all situations to sharpen your skills and causes you to do some upfront homework in order to prepare you for success in these conversations. These approaches get you to that end state by including everyday hints and suggestions.

The method is:

PICK – Set yourself up for where and how to begin

PREP – Do your homework and create a list of topics/questions

GO – Start with small efforts to introduce your voice

1. PICK:

In order to start tawking in public, you need to plan for your forays into this process, so that you have a short script that takes the initial fears out of it. Start small – pick out an upcoming event to start your journey. It can be an outing with friends to have a cup of cawfee or it could be a small team meeting at work. What I recommend is a social outing, a party or gathering where people will be milling, and small talk will be the mode of conversation. Some suggestions:

A - The Social Event: This is the one situation that most training participants wanted to try out first, and the one that I recommend as well.

B - Meeting with Friends: If you're meeting friends for a meal or drinks, think about who will be attending, and whether you know about something one or two of them are dealing with, working on.

C - The Work Meeting: If it's a work meeting, think about the subject of the meeting, and if this is an opportunity to raise or address other issues.

2. PREP:

You must do some homework, some preparation prior to the event. You need to develop topics or questions to have at the ready, so that you do not have to think on your feet. You just have to 'read' from your memorized script (Ready List), comprised of a few quick questions, statements.

Start by thinking about something that could be discussed at that event and develop a couple of questions around that topic. Thinking about the event in advance, and doing your homework, also allows you to consciously think about the attendees in detail.

This is a big benefit as it makes you more comfortable at the actual event. I found that this preparation tricks your mind into thinking that you already have met these people, and it takes away some of the shock value of being in a room with strangers.

HOMEWORK ASSIGNMENT

Develop a couple of questions or talking points in advance, that could be generic to anyone, or specific to a particular attendee. Depending on the circumstances, you may need to do a bit of research into the event purpose, location, or to find out about some of the attendees, honorees, etc.

You need to write down the list of questions, talking points, so that you memorize them verbatim. Again, you are trying to reduce the fear factor as much as possible, so memorizing this Ready List is the best plan.

It's perfectly okay if your questions are more fluff than substance at the beginning. In fact, it's probably best if the Ready List is initially stacked with simple, non-complex thoughts and issues, so that you are not creating a huge follow-on discussion requirement. The questions and statements with more substance will follow as you increase your comfort level.

And until you reach that comfort level, start slowly. Asking people a concise question about themselves is magical – people love to talk about themselves. Your interest in that person will be seen as very positive in their eyes, and without having to speak too much, you are connecting with that person in an affirmative, friendly manner. This will also make you more confident about hearing the sound of your voice out loud.

MAIN HINTS: SMALL AND SIMPLE!

Make these questions or statements very short – you want to be able to ask something or state something very quickly, using just a few words. You want to be able to hear your voice in public, but at first, you need to only speak in short spurts with small words. If not, you'll scare the hell out of yourself – and I speak from sweaty experience on this issue.

How To Develop Your Ready List Of Sample Questions, Talking Points:

Your goal is to develop at least two or three questions or statements to use for your PREP. You should not be struggling with how to begin your homework to create your Ready List of talking points or questions, as it is a much simpler task.

Consider the following things to get your homework going to develop your Ready List of talking points:

If it's a Social Event, think about the host/hostess of the event:

- Who are they, and formulate associated questions

- Ask them what they do for a living, or do they have any special interests

- Are they famous for some specific reasons, such as writing a best-selling book, engaging in civic projects, or involved in front-page events

- Steer away from infamous events as that may raise embarrassing moments for the host/hostess, and you

More topics for the Social Event:

- If the party is being held in an event-space or house, find out if there is any special history tied to the catering hall, building, community, and ask the hosts about it

- Ask why they selected this charity, this program, etc.

- Ask attendees how they know the hosts

- Ask someone what they do, or if they are working on any special projects, programs

- Ask them what are the top two issues facing their company

- Is xxx their hometown? (Find out what their hometown is and ask them about it.)

- Ask if they have any plans for a new book; similarly, ask what the muse for their last book was

- Ask them if they have any plans for their next vacation

Topics for the meeting with your friends:

- Ask about their new job, promotion, what are they working on

- Find out about the attendees you do not have a personal connection to, and ask a question about something they are passionate about

- Ask a question about prior information you know about them, such as their families, where they live

- Mention a local charity that needs help and suggest you all volunteer together

- Ask if anyone has a recommendation for a dentist, painter, gardener

- If a friend or other participant recently renovated their home, ask how they arranged for their redo

If it's a work meeting, think about the meeting lead:

- Who is she/he

- What do they do

- Think if you have any people connections in common with the leader

More topics for the work meeting:

- Ask if there is a timeline for the project

- Ask how success will be measured

- Ask if there are additional timeframes, financial implications or constraints

- Inquire if there is an opportunity for other team members to help

- If applicable to the venue/meeting, introduce a suggestion you have for improving a work product or process

EXTRA CREDIT POINTS:

Okay, here is my gift to you that ALWAYS gives you a connection to the attendees, with limited homework. It is my GO-TO Topic that never fails when everything else seems wrong...

SPORTS!

Don't let this scare you – even if you know NOTHING about sports, it doesn't matter. With a limited amount of newly found knowledge from perusing the sports pages or listening to sportscasters on the local news, you can introduce this topic when nothing else you prepared seems applicable.

Preparation for SPORTS discussions:

- Depending on the time of year, pick an active sport.

- Think locally – what's the status of your local sports teams, any controversial issues.

- Newsworthy issues – what's in the sports pages this week – i.e., is there a change in leadership, such as a coach being hired or an athlete in the news for something extraordinary, either within her/his sport, or in their personal lives.

- Develop a question or a statement based on any of the above.

- Based on your comfort level, you may need to read up on the issue you select, but not too much.

- If you are a novice to the sports pages, frame your issue as a question, asking the party goers for help understanding it. For example, "why did the owner of the xxx sports team hire a new General Manager" or "who will win the Sweet 16." You really don't need to know too much to introduce the subject, and in framing it as a question, you are seeking information.

- Remember with short questions and small words, you'll start hearing your voice in a crowd – and using a Sports item will get everyone engaged in something you raise in the conversation. This is always a crowd pleaser and a fail-safe topic.

3. GO:

This is where the Simple Steps come in – you have to start slowly! You've picked your first event wisely, you also have a couple of questions and points memorized, and now, you have to pick just one thing to say. No, I mean it – ONE THING ONLY! And then you need to concentrate on hearing what you are saying out loud, in front of a crowd of people. As you continue this process, start adding more you into the conversation(s), as you feel comfortable doing, using the same preps.

The more you practice this, the easier it gets. I also found myself more engaged and involved in topics of conversation I never had a prior interest in.

FOLLOW-UP PROCEDURES

Once you start to get comfortable hearing your voice out loud, you need to start incorporating this method into your daily life. And truthfully, the more you exercise this ask a simple question portion in just one-on-one chance meetings with a friend or a colleague or a fellow patron in the grocery store, the more comfortable you will be in hearing your voice. And speaking well in public is key to your metamorphosis.

These 'hallway' discussions where you start to hear your voice in a non-fearful manner, are just what you need to start hearing your voice out loud. Ask the cashier at the grocery store something, ask the Mail Carriers about their day, ask your neighbors about their jobs. The more you hear yourself talking out loud, the easier it gets – and then it gets fun! Some call this 'Small Talk' but small talk IS the art of conversation. Once you master this, you can take on any challenge.

Some additional suggestions:

Rehearse your telephone speech before dialing. Write down your thoughts or questions in advance of the call. Practice assertively saying an entire thought, making sure you don't raise your voice as if you are asking a question if you are making a statement.

Speak in short sentences in order to get your full point across – and try to limit the number of sentences to a few concise ones.

Practice speaking in front of a mirror to get comfortable with the sound of your voice.

At social settings, force yourself to walk up to a loud gathering – at first, you don't have to add to the conversation, just be part of the group. Enjoy the livelier interactions, and soon you'll find that these more active groupings are more fun.

Trouble with confidence? Try pretending you're acting, and you have to enter 'the stage' pretending to be someone else. Imagine you're playing a role – it may help to get you started.

Ask questions that you already know the answers to so that you are more confident of engaging with the group.

If you're afraid of social situations, such as dancing in public, take dance lessons. You'll only need a few instructions to make yourself more at ease, and you'll realize that you're a better dancer than you think.

For the OOPS Situations:

Although I highly recommend that you never get into this type of situation, especially when starting out on the right path to address your Dirty Laundry, it is possible that you are foisted into an **OOPS situation** for a spur-of-the-moment event. If you want to jump-in, try adding more comments at first rather than starting out as an experienced conversationalist.

You can begin by adding a "really" or "what was that like" in an inquisitive, interested tone, when someone states something, and then let them react to you. It shows you are attentive and engaged in what they said, and they will react positively and warmly, but don't make a habit of winging it without doing your homework and creating your talking points. This can backfire, especially if you start to get smug and overconfident without doing your needed homework. Never forget that the goal is to become confident in hearing the sound of your voice in public, and the method I created will help you do that by establishing a solid foundation rather than a precarious platform.

CHAPTER 7: ADDITIONAL POINTS

IPO – Individual Power Organization:

You control 100% of your actions. You also have as much authority as you choose to take responsibility for.

Many women who fall into a subservient role may think it is not within their power to make a difference, or not within their abilities to change their situation. That is a trap that first has to be recognized in order to be able to address it.

It's Too Late for Me to Change:

Think where you'll be in 10 years if you don't start to reach for your goals today. The momentum gets stronger and easier once you start the journey. Never too early, and never too late, to control your fate. Seasoning makes everything better and tastier!

Don't allow any barriers or biases to cloud your improvement. If stuck, think short term goals (where do I want to be in six months, one year, or three years).

Goal Planning:

* Identify specific requirements needed to obtain your goal.

* Training and Education are required, no matter what the subject is.

* Seek guidance from others.

* Ask questions.

* Ask someone to be your mentor.

* **READ, READ, READ!** I made a conscious decision years ago to concentrate my reading on non-fiction works, mostly self-improvement books and newspapers. Just recently I started to include fiction back in my reading lists because I enjoy it and do learn from it as well, but I still concentrate on non-fiction. You need to figure out what is best for you.

The Worst Lie:

The worst lie is that You Can Have It All. No one can, so be sure of what you want and what you are willing to give up or sacrifice, to get what you do want. Make conscious decisions to dedicate your efforts to reach your goals. Seek and gain commitment and support from people in your life who may be affected by your goals and decisions.

♦♦♦

GOING FORWARD AND FINAL THOUGHTS

Here is the final part of this training. Whether it is addressing your Doormat items or improving your public speaking skills, you need to take advantage of any and every interaction with people to ensure that you continue to improve.

And here's another confession – I still practice this every single day! I review my actions and interactions after I attend any function, meeting, party, after phone conversations, etc., and replay the situations in my head. As proof, to this day, I never make a call to request service or to solicit information, without first developing a talking points list.

These reviews are to make sure I was effective, that I contributed, added value, achieved my goal for the interaction, and that no one, including myself, attempted or succeeded in negatively impacting me. Occasionally I will also seek input from others, as an additional check and balance.

Based on my assessments of these events, I readjust how I will address similar situations in the future. I try to do this after every encounter, even a trip to the store. I think about what I could have done better, how I was perceived, and check for any Dirty Laundry I addressed or missed.

I am, and will continue to be **A WORK IN PROGRESS**, and I hope you will be, too.

Made in the USA
Coppell, TX
04 November 2022